W9-BAV-686

Amy Hogeboom is also the author of

Horses and How To Draw Them

Dogs and How To Draw Them

Forest Animals and How To Draw Them

Wild Animals and How To Draw Them

Boats and How To Draw Them

Cats and How To Draw Them

Birds and How To Draw Them

Sea Animals and How To Draw Them

AMY HOGEBOOM

Familiar Animals

and how to draw them

THE VANGUARD PRESS • NEW YORK

Published simultaneously in Canada by the Copp Clark Co., Ltd.

Acknowledgment: Photographs of the Turkey and Donkey are printed by courtesy of Ewing Galloway; those of the Hen and Sheep, courtesy of Philip D. Gendreau; those of the Cow and Goat, courtesy of Black Star; those of the Horse and the Cat, courtesy of Frederic Lewis; that of the Pig, courtesy of Harold M. Lambert Studios.

Manufactured in the United States of America

CONTENTS

THE HORSE

The finest Horses originally came from Arabia. They are the saddle and racing horses. For the heavy work on a farm a sturdier horse is used. Big truck horses are usually Percherons and are the largest and strongest of any. Mustangs are the small, partly wild horses of our western plains. Pinto is a western name for the small spotted horse of that country. Some of these horses are so small that they are called ponies. The smallest horse of all is the little Shetland pony, the stocky little fellow all children love.

The Horse

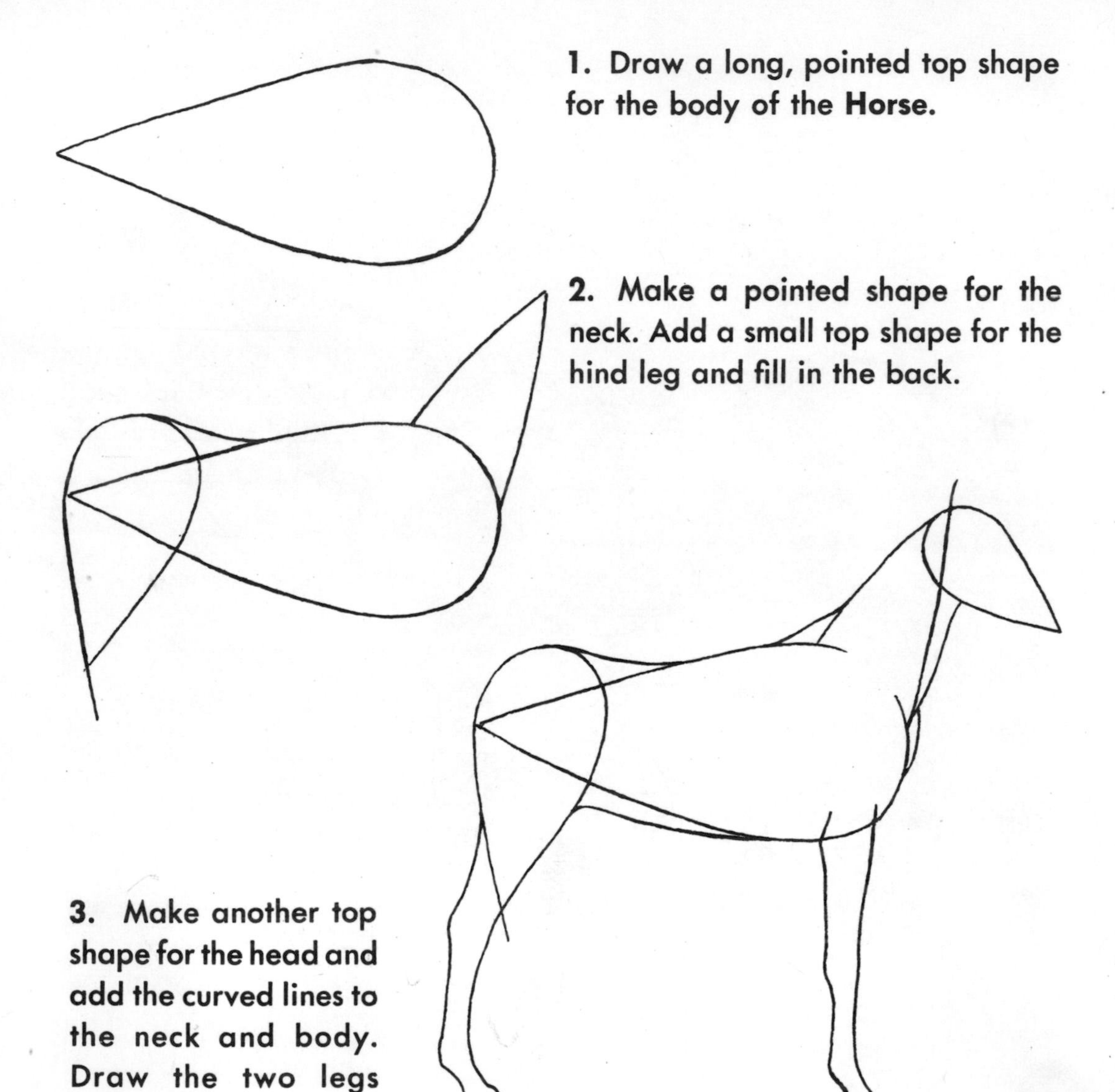

1. Draw a long, pointed top shape for the body of the **Horse.**

2. Make a pointed shape for the neck. Add a small top shape for the hind leg and fill in the back.

3. Make another top shape for the head and add the curved lines to the neck and body. Draw the two legs shown here.

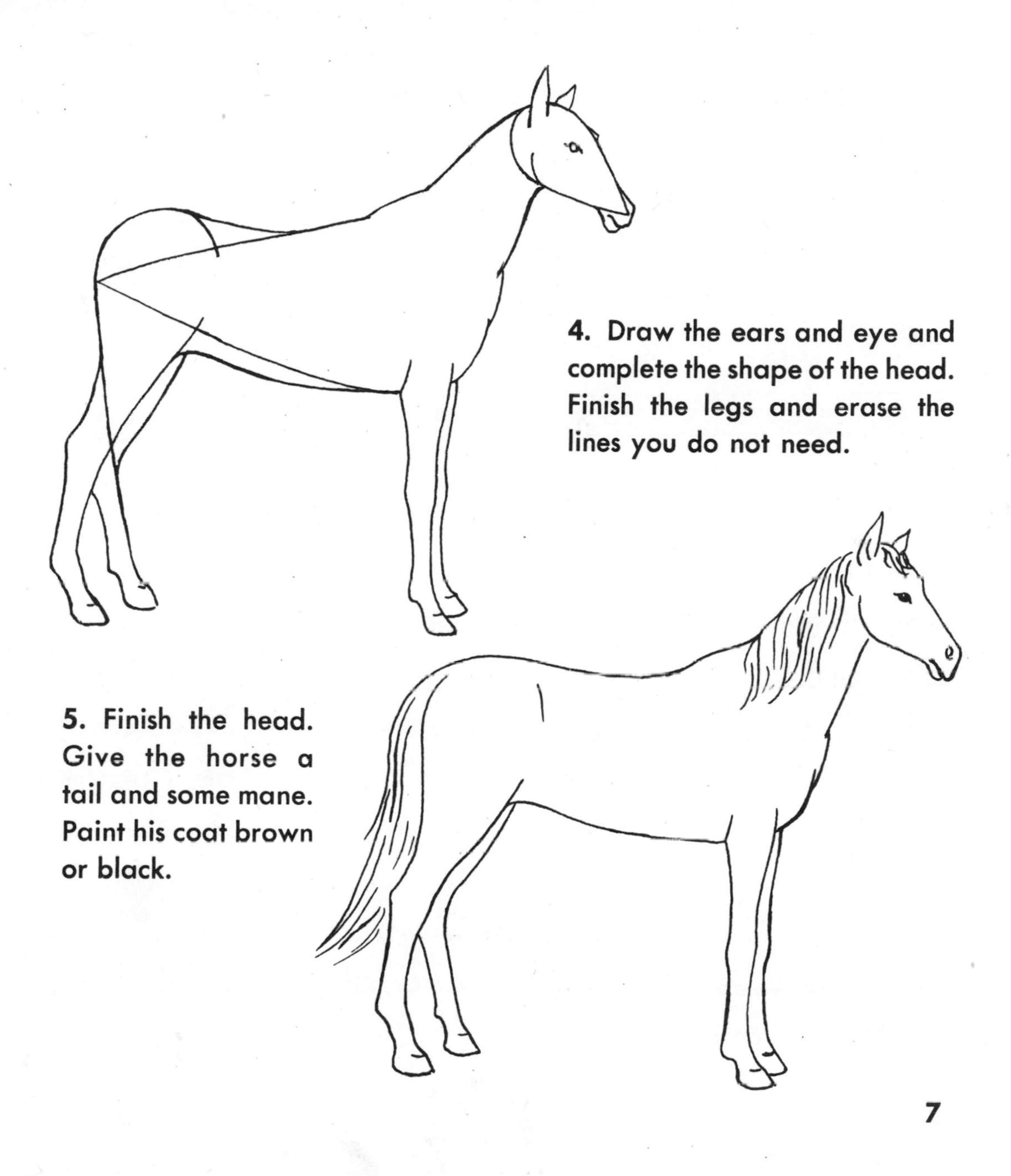

4. Draw the ears and eye and complete the shape of the head. Finish the legs and erase the lines you do not need.

5. Finish the head. Give the horse a tail and some mane. Paint his coat brown or black.

THE COW

The Holstein Cow is the large black and white one you often see. Jersey and Guernsey cows are smaller and are a soft brown color or spotted brown and white. They came originally from the Islands of Jersey and Guernsey in the English Channel. The famous Texas Longhorns were brought over by the Spaniards long ago, to that part of the country. Shorthorns were the cows used in the north. Cows furnish us with good, strong leather and also give us milk, butter, cheese, and beef.

The Cow

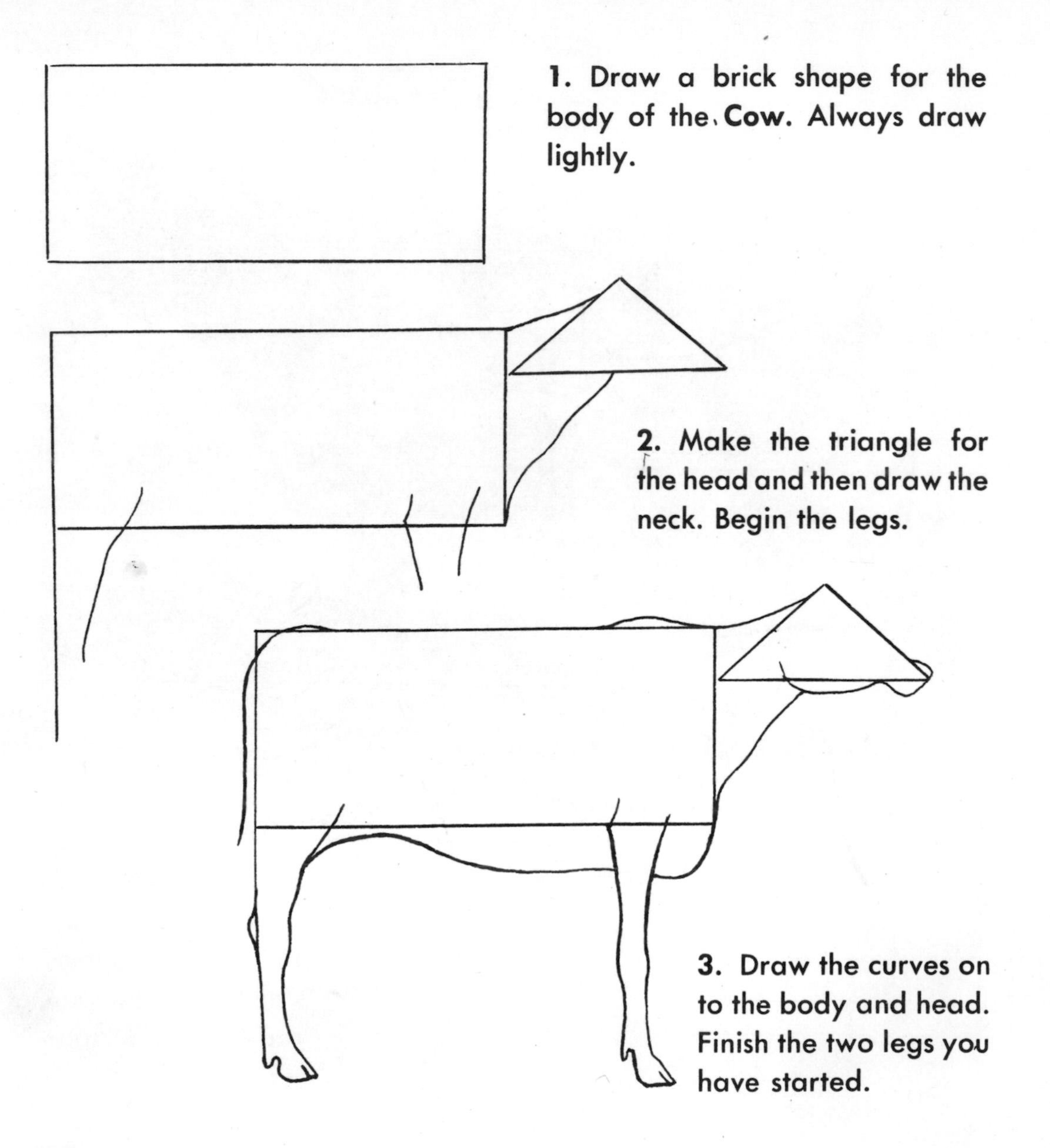

1. Draw a brick shape for the body of the **Cow.** Always draw lightly.

2. Make the triangle for the head and then draw the neck. Begin the legs.

3. Draw the curves on to the body and head. Finish the two legs you have started.

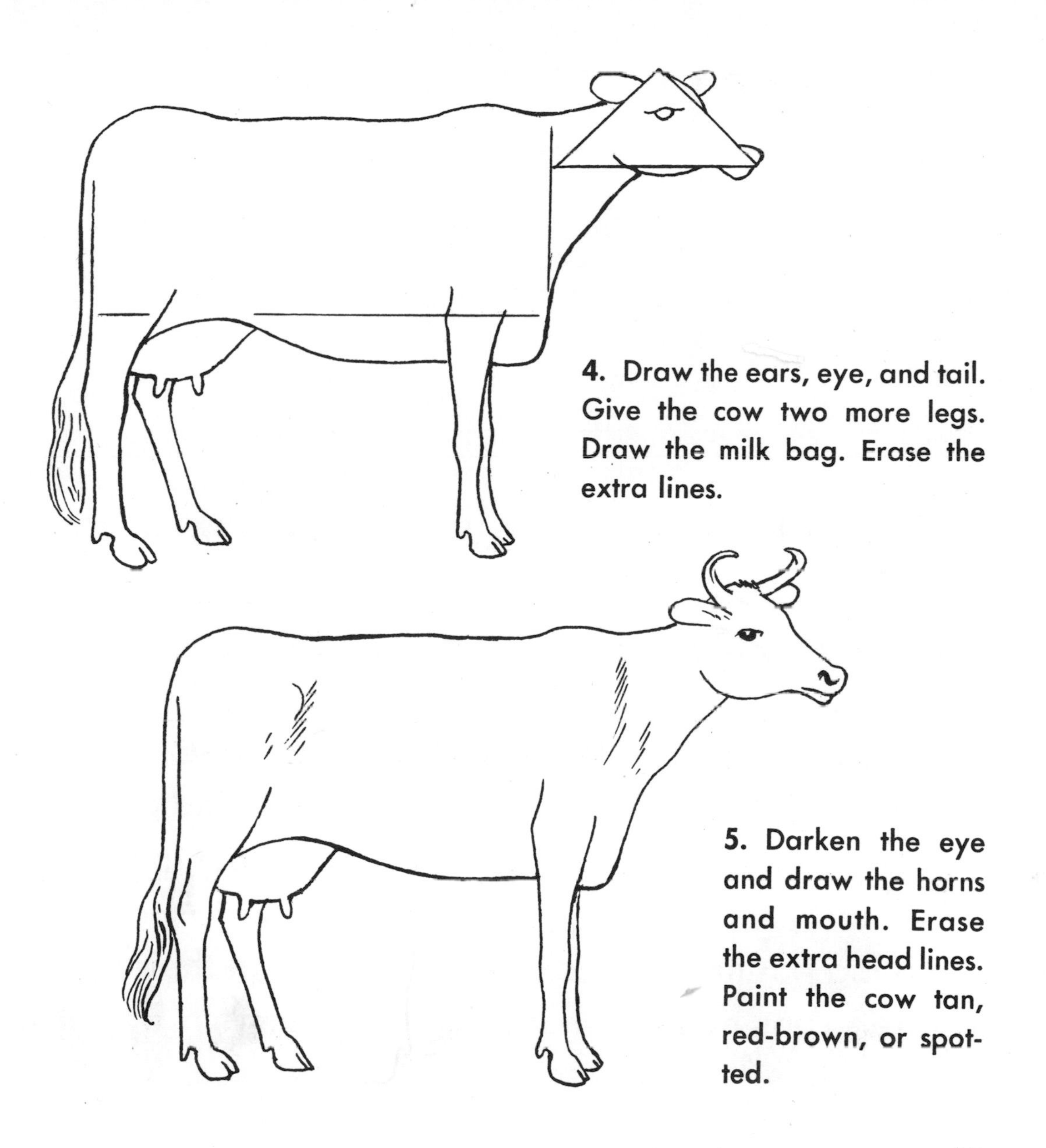

4. Draw the ears, eye, and tail. Give the cow two more legs. Draw the milk bag. Erase the extra lines.

5. Darken the eye and draw the horns and mouth. Erase the extra head lines. Paint the cow tan, red-brown, or spotted.

THE HEN

It is great fun to feed the Chickens on a farm. The minute they see the farmer with the pan of corn they come running from everywhere: from under the fences, over the fences, from behind the bushes, and every place you can think of. Long ago, when there were no alarm clocks, many people depended on the roosters to wake them up in the morning, but in these times sunrise is too early for most people to waken. On a big poultry farm, chickens are kept in their own chicken runs and are not allowed to scratch up the flower beds.

The Hen

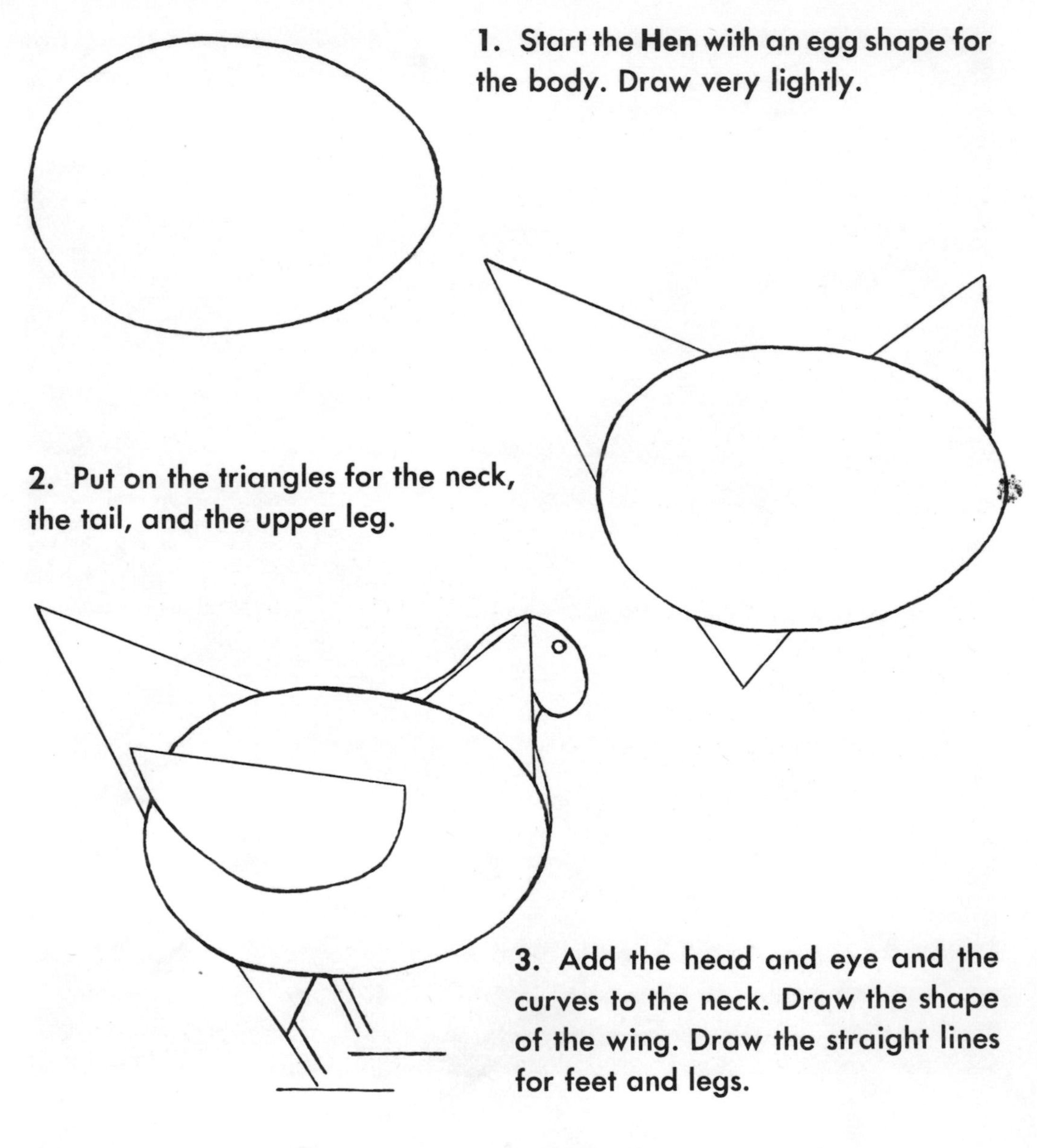

1. Start the **Hen** with an egg shape for the body. Draw very lightly.

2. Put on the triangles for the neck, the tail, and the upper leg.

3. Add the head and eye and the curves to the neck. Draw the shape of the wing. Draw the straight lines for feet and legs.

4. Draw the bill and begin the claws. Make the feathers on wing and tail. Erase the extra lines.

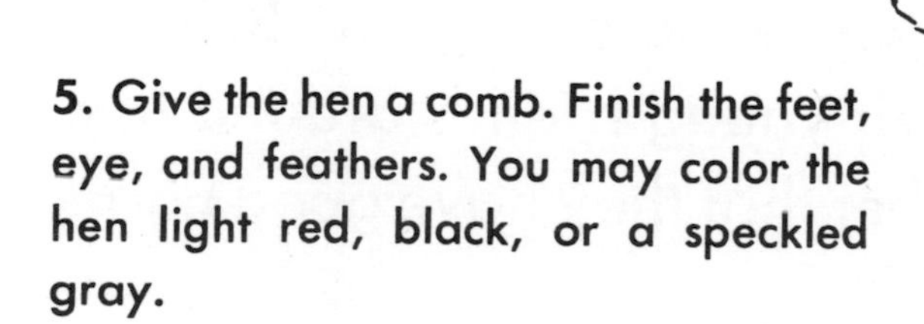

5. Give the hen a comb. Finish the feet, eye, and feathers. You may color the hen light red, black, or a speckled gray.

THE GOAT

The Goat is a hardy, tough little animal. He climbs over rocks and stone walls and loves to stand on some high place where he can look about. He often runs away because he likes to ramble where he has no business to be, and he will take a bite out of almost anything just to see what it is made of. When he gets really hungry he will come home again. Billy or Nanny willingly pull their young friends around in a cart; but always remember that they have good horns to use.

The Goat

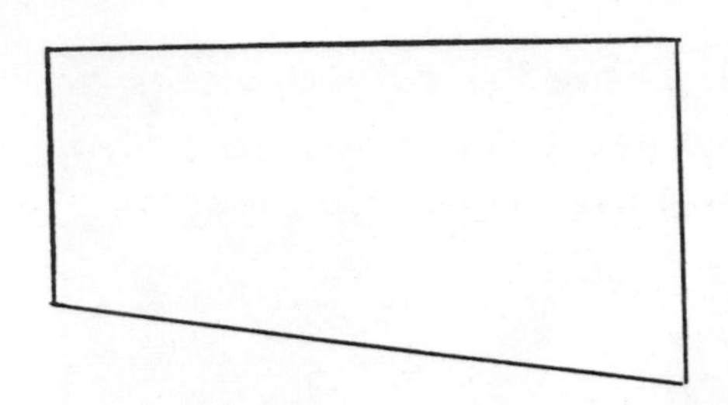

1. Begin with this uneven block shape for the **Goat's** body. Draw lightly.

2. Draw the shape for the narrow head. Then make the neck. Begin the legs.

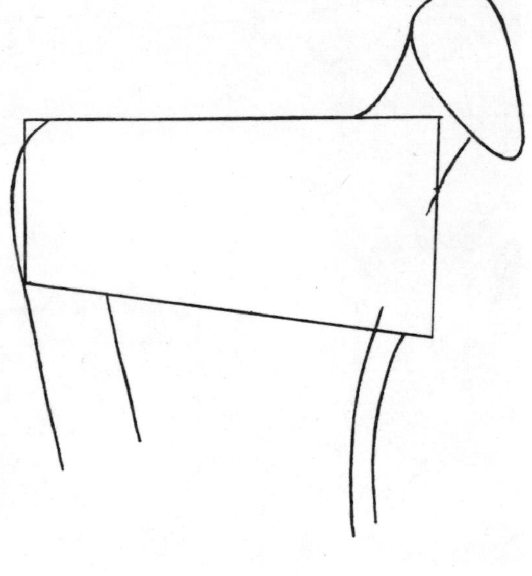

3. Add the horns. Add the curve to the chest. Finish the legs.

4. Draw the curved pieces on the head. Make the ears, eye, and tail. Erase the extra lines.

5. Finish Billy's nose and give him his whiskers. Use short lines for his rough fur. He may be white, black, or spotted.

THE PIG

Most farmers will tell you that a Pig will keep clean if he has the opportunity. Modern pigsties are well furnished with clean straw and plenty of fresh water. Even the little piglets keep their faces nearly clean. It is too bad that their eating manners have not improved as well, for they still stick their snouts right into the food and grunt when they eat. If another pig gets in their way at the feeding trough they still yelp, "Oinck, oinck!" and push him rudely to one side.

The Pig

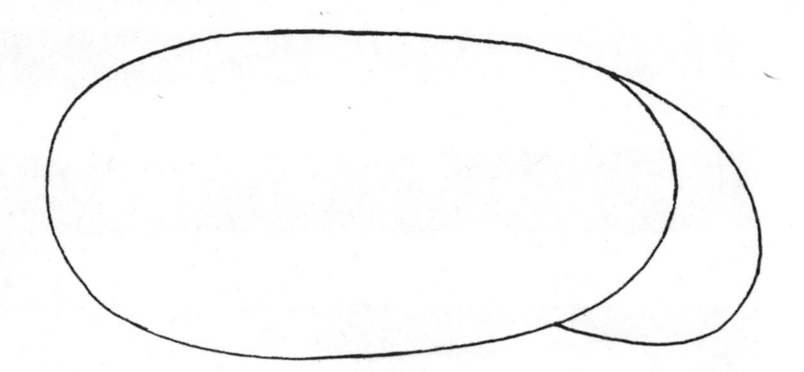

1. Start the **Pig** drawing with a large watermelon shape. Add the curved piece for the head.

2. Put the snout on the head. Begin the legs.

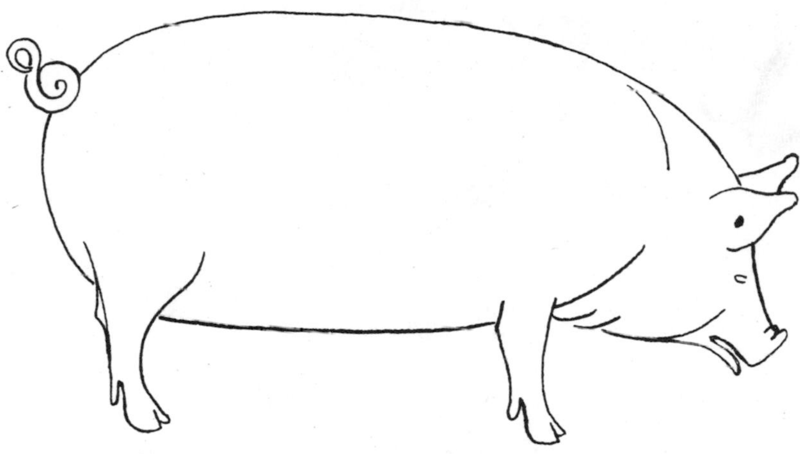

3. Give the pig a tail, an eye, and ears. Finish the snout and the two legs already started. Put some wrinkles in his neck. Erase the extra lines.

4. Now make the other two legs. Paint the pig black or spotted if you wish.

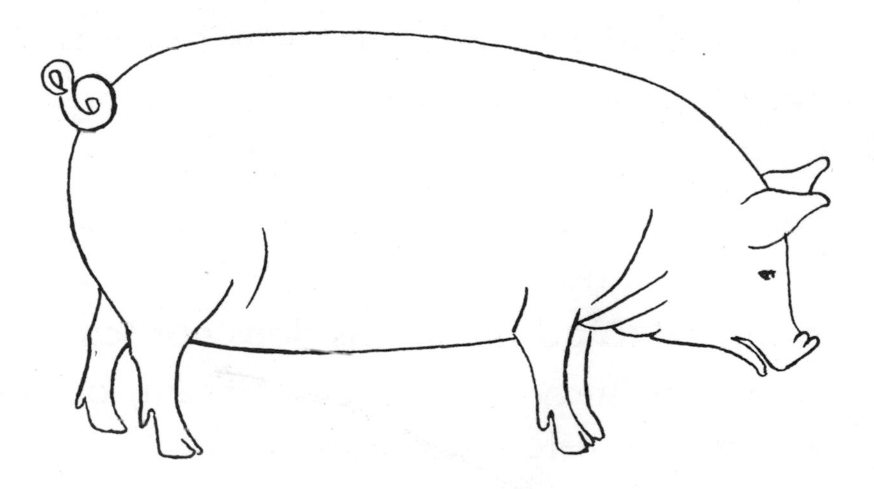

THE TURKEY

Our barnyard Turkey is the wild turkey of Mexico and the Southwest. The father turkey cock is still rather wild and does not like anyone to come too near him or his family. When anything disturbs him, he begins his gobble, gobble sound, roughs up his feathers, drags his wings, and spreads out his big tail. When he is angry, his head and wattles change from red to purple. If this does not scare his enemies away, he may try to rush at them, but he will turn and run swiftly if it is necessary.

The Turkey

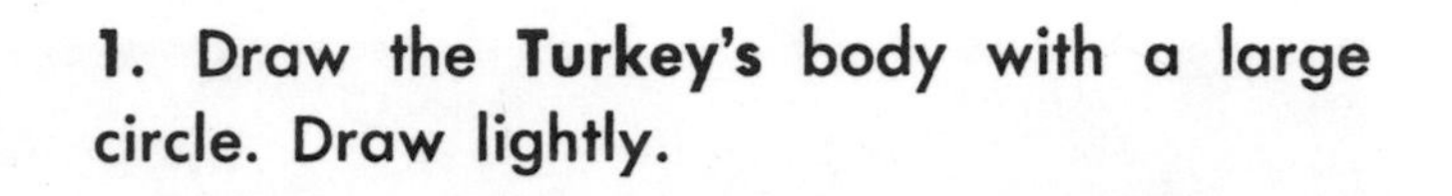

1. Draw the **Turkey's** body with a large circle. Draw lightly.

2. Make a large top shape for the tail. Draw a smaller top shape for the head.

3. Draw the two curves for the wing. Begin the neck and one leg.

4. Put in an eye. Finish his neck by adding the wattles. Finish one leg and erase the extra lines. Start the feather line around the tail.

5. Add another foot and finish the feathers. Color the head, neck, and wattles red and make the feathers brown.

THE CAT

Cats are very independent animals. That is why it is so difficult to teach them tricks, but in some ways they are smarter than dogs. They often learn by themselves how to open door latches and turn on water faucets. You cannot force them to do these tricks, but if you watch them you will see them do many clever things. Originally, cats came from warm countries, and for this reason they should always have a warm place in which to sleep. They catch mice for sport but seldom eat them, and they will hunt just as well if properly fed.

The Cat

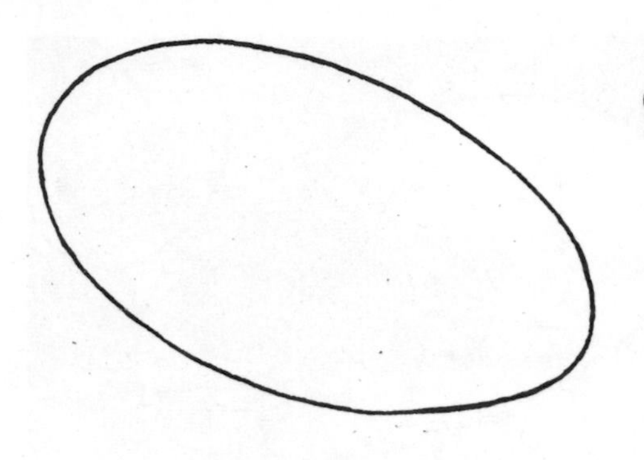

1. Draw a long oval shape for the Cat's body.

2. Add a rounded shape for the head and then make the neck. Begin the legs.

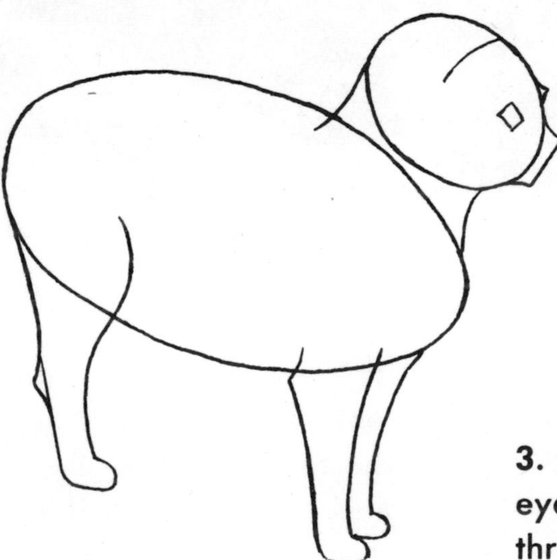

3. Add the nose to the head. Place the eye and a line for the ears. Finish the three legs you have begun.

4. Add a tail and a fourth leg. Draw the mouth, eye, and ears. Erase the extra lines.

5. Give your cat some whiskers and toes. Use short, light lines for the fur and make stripes if you wish.

THE DONKEY

Donkeys are known for their stubbornness, although they really are patient, faithful animals. Usually they have good reasons for their actions. They are often given loads which are too heavy for them, and when this happens they just say, "Hee, haw! Hee, haw!" and will not budge an inch. When Pedro, the donkey, has a boy or girl to carry on his back or drag in a cart, it is plain that he likes his burden. In the mountains, on steep narrow paths, it is best to ride a donkey or a mule.

The Donkey

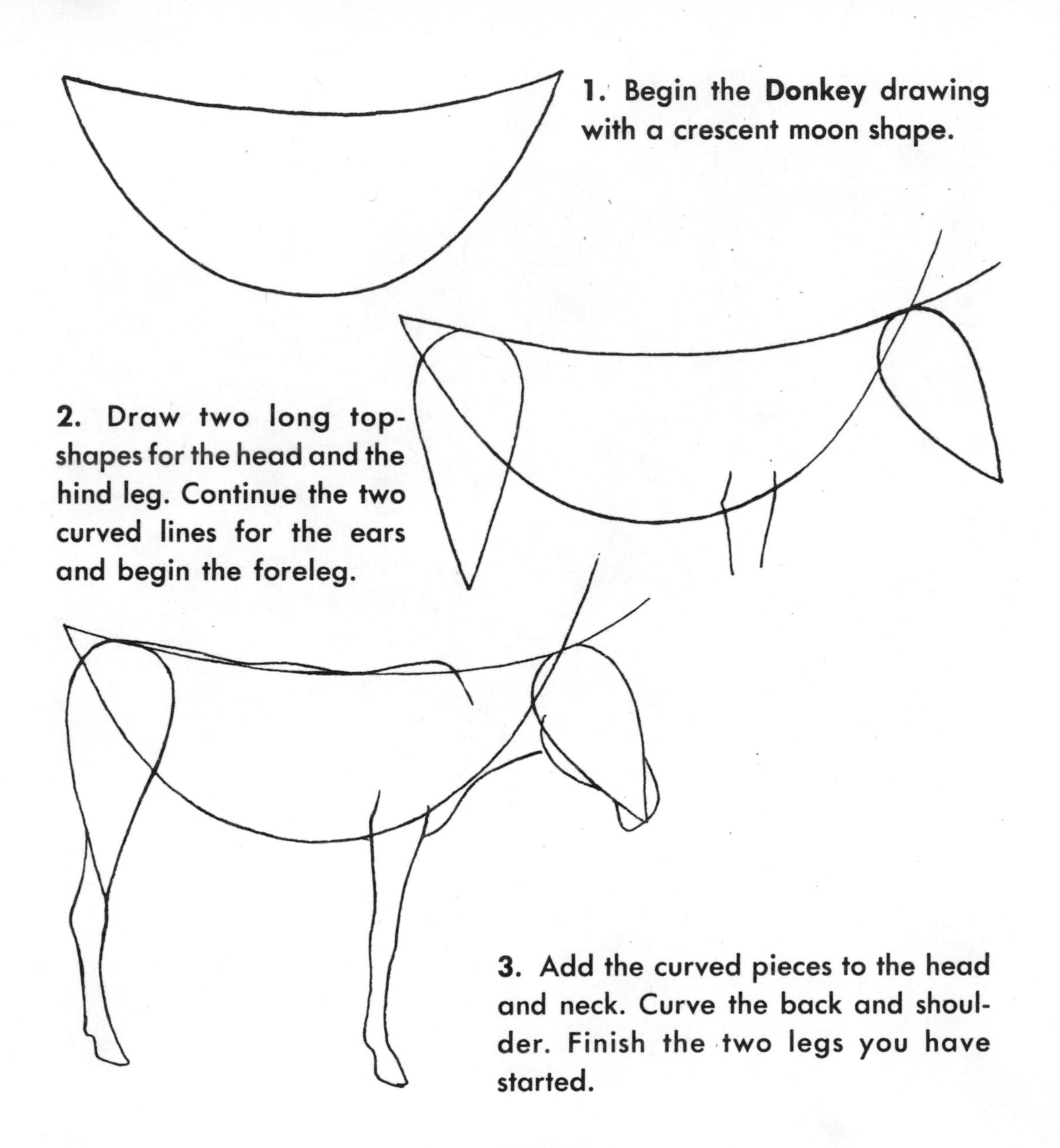

1. Begin the **Donkey** drawing with a crescent moon shape.

2. Draw two long top-shapes for the head and the hind leg. Continue the two curved lines for the ears and begin the foreleg.

3. Add the curved pieces to the head and neck. Curve the back and shoulder. Finish the two legs you have started.

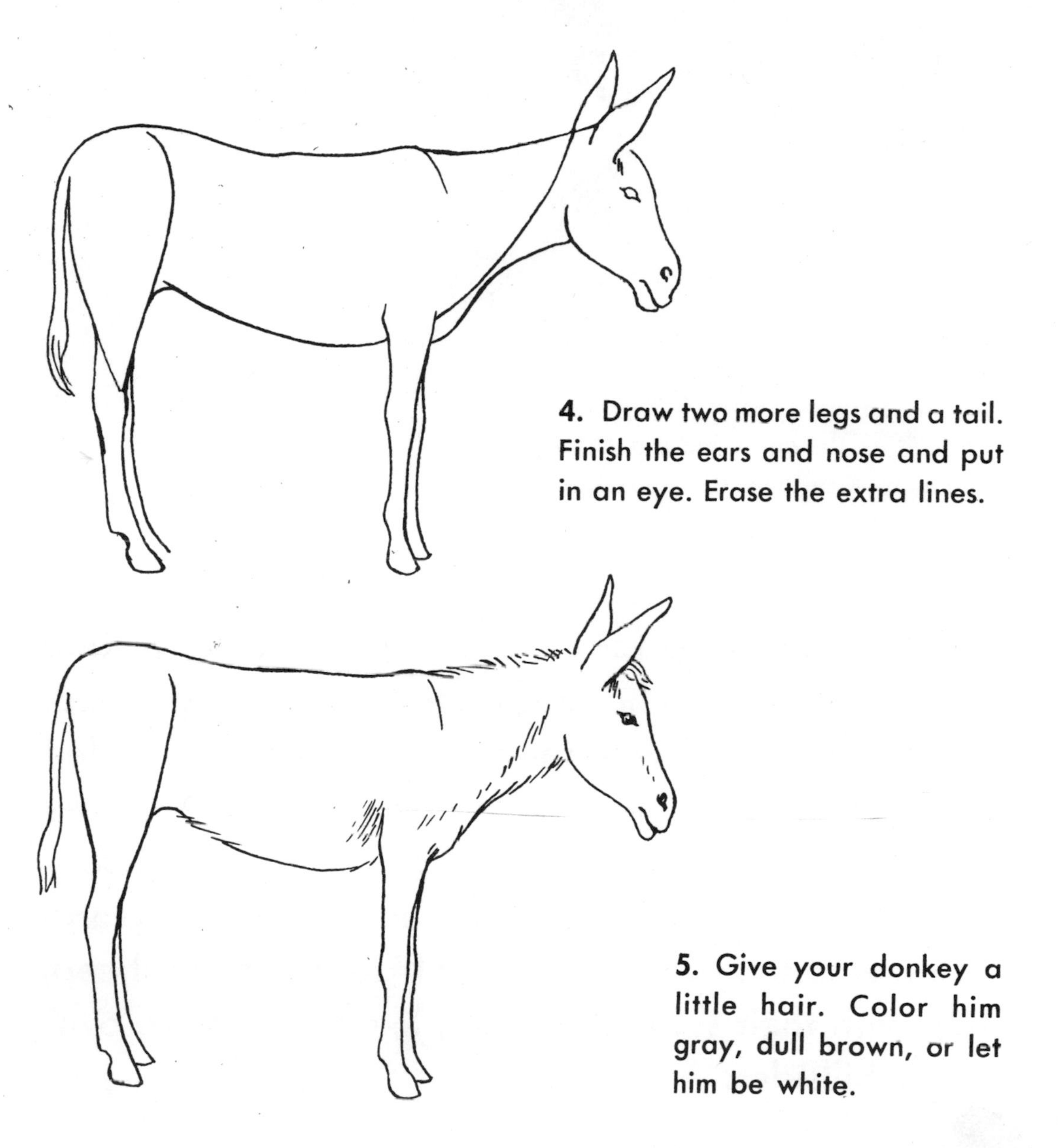

4. Draw two more legs and a tail. Finish the ears and nose and put in an eye. Erase the extra lines.

5. Give your donkey a little hair. Color him gray, dull brown, or let him be white.

THE SHEEP

Sheep are very necessary to us. We depend upon the wool of the sheep for clothes to keep us warm and for the blankets on our beds. Lambs are young sheep. The father sheep, with their curved horns, are called rams. A flock of sheep have one leader which they follow blindly, even into danger. Our wild Rocky Mountain sheep are noted for their ability to leap and climb where no other animal will go. The farm sheep, too, with their sure little hoofs, like to scramble over rocky hillsides.

The Sheep

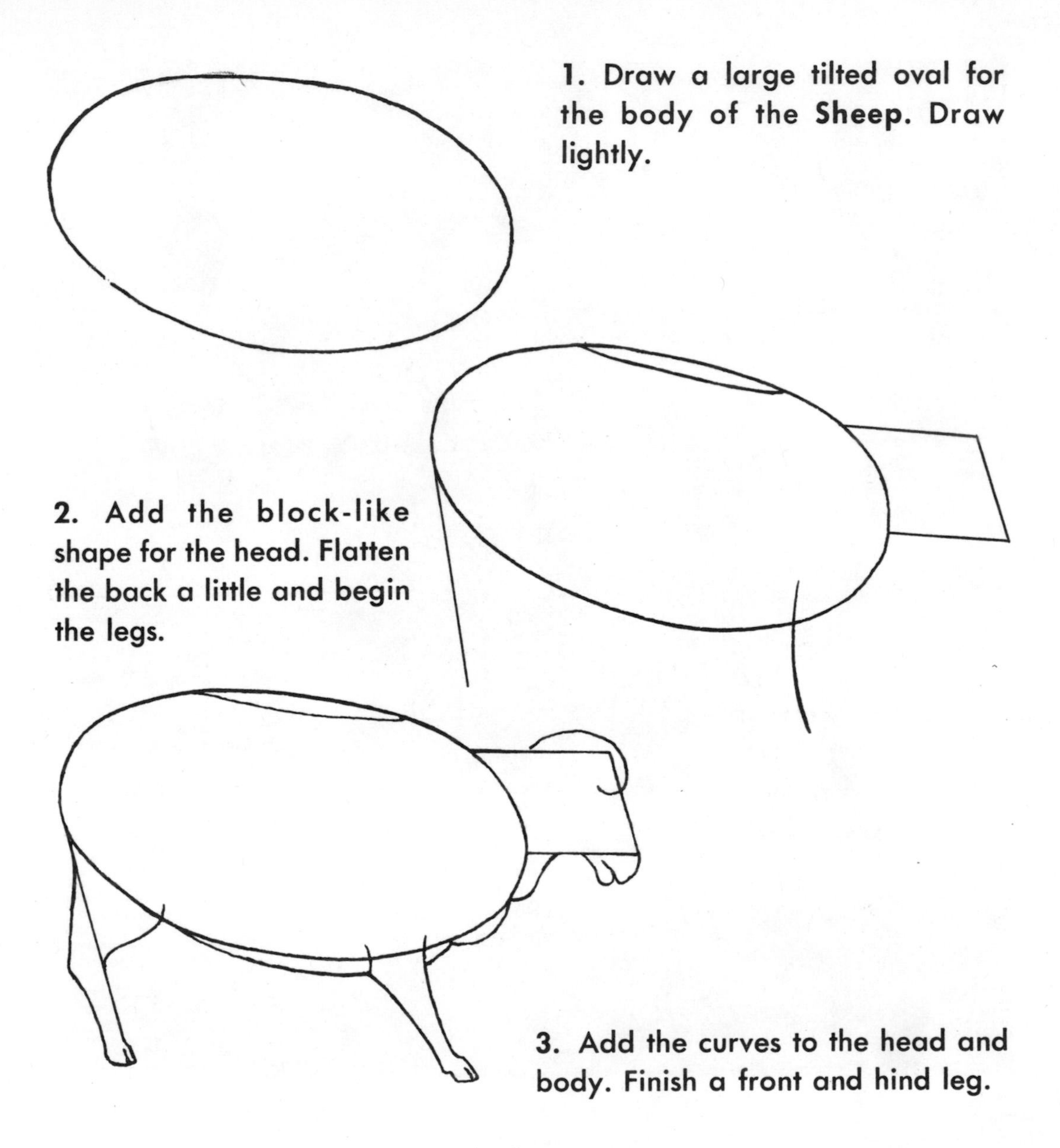

1. Draw a large tilted oval for the body of the **Sheep.** Draw lightly.

2. Add the block-like shape for the head. Flatten the back a little and begin the legs.

3. Add the curves to the head and body. Finish a front and hind leg.

4. Make two more legs and a tail. Draw the eye. Erase the lines not needed. Make a wavy outline.

5. Give the sheep a woolly look with light, wiggly lines. You may make the sheep black or white.